WHICH ONE OF THESE COULD

EAT YOUR

FLESH

IN TWO DAYS?

Turn the page to find out the answer!

BIOHAZARD

BIOHAZARD

BIOHAZARD

ANSWER: STREP

That's short for Group A Streptococcus.

In rare cases, strep gets under the skin and causes a disease called necrotizing fasciitis. People call it the "flesh-eating disease"— and for good reason. Strep can kill your flesh. Strep bacteria move through your body at an inch (2.5 cm) an hour. People with necrotizing fasciitis need to get to the hospital quickly. The disease can kill you in two days.

As for the dinosaur, it's a velociraptor. And it's extinct. So what are you worried about?

Book design Red Herring Design/NYC

Library of Congress Cataloging-in-Publication Data
Tilden, Thomasine E. Lewis, 1958–
Help! what's eating my flesh? : runaway staph and strep infections! /
by Thomasine E. Lewis Tilden.
p. cm. — (24/7: science behind the scenes)
Includes bibliographical references and index.
ISBN-13: 978-0-531-12073-6 (lib. bdg.)   978-0-531-18738-8 (pbk.)
ISBN-10: 0-531-12073-2 (lib. bdg.)   0-531-18738-1 (pbk.)
1. Staphylococcal infections—Juvenile literature. I. Title.
RC116.S8T55 2006
616.9'2—dc22   2006005871

© 2008 Scholastic Inc.
All rights reserved. Published by Franklin Watts, an imprint of Scholastic Inc.

Published simultaneously in Canada. Printed in the United States of America.

SCHOLASTIC, FRANKLIN WATTS, and associated logos are trademarks and/or registered trademarks of Scholastic Inc.
1 2 3 4 5 6 7 8 9 10 R   17 16 15 14 13 12 11 10 09 08

HELP! WHAT'S EATING MY FLESH?

Runaway Staph and Strep Infections!

Thomasine E. Lewis Tilden

WARNING: This book contains some really gross facts and photos. Turn the page at your own risk. **READER DISCRETION IS ADVISED.**

Franklin Watts
An Imprint of Scholastic Inc.
New York • Toronto • London • Auckland • Sydney
Mexico City • New Delhi • Hong Kong
Danbury, Connecticut

CONTENTS

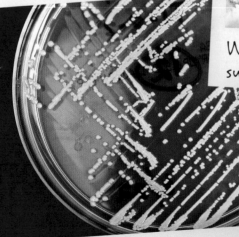

TRUE-LIFE CASE FILES!

These cases are 100% real. Find out how doctors handled some skin-crawling diseases.

15 Case #1:
The Terrible Tale of the Flesh-Eating Disease
A minor injury turns into a deadly infection. Can a doctor stop the bacteria before they kill their host?

In California, could a tiny scratch kill a man?

27 Case #2:
No Time to Lose
A woman survives surgery—but gets a terrible infection. She'll need emergency surgery to save her life.

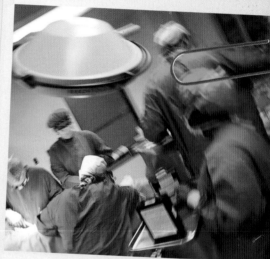

Will a woman in Los Angeles survive a post-surgery infection?

35 Case #3:
Help! I Can't Breathe!
It seemed like just a bad case of the flu. So why is the patient now fighting for his life?

Will tests reveal a killer in Woodland Hills, CA?

Here's some more infectious stuff about bacteria for your reading pleasure.

Bacteria are the most common living things on earth. You carry them wherever you go.

MEDICAL 411

They live on your hands and under your feet. They hide in your mouth, nose, and eyes. Most of them wouldn't hurt a flea. But if conditions are just right, they can cause big problems.

IN THIS SECTION:

▶ how infectious disease specialists really talk;
▶ how germs can invade your body;
▶ and who else works in the lab.

Spreading Germs

Infectious disease specialists have their own way of talking. Find out what their vocabulary means.

bacteria
(bak-TEER-ee-a) single-celled life-forms found in the air, soil, or water, which can cause disease in humans

A lot of kids in her class are sick. I'm sure there are bacteria everywhere.

This case could be serious. Let's call in an infectious disease doctor.

infectious disease doctor
(in-FEK-shuhss duh-ZEEZ DOK-tur) a doctor who specializes in diagnosing and treating all kinds of infections

She's got a serious infection. Get her on antibiotics right away.

infection
(in-FEK-shun) sickness caused when bacteria or viruses invade the body

antibiotic
(AN-tee-bye-OT-ik) a drug that kills bacteria and helps treat infections

> This kind of **staph** is resistant to most antibiotics.

staph
(staf) common bacteria carried on skin and in noses. It's short for *Staphylococcus*. When it gets inside the next layer of skin, it can cause a painful, red skin infection. If it gets deeper, it can require surgery.

resistant
(ri-ZIS-tent) able to fight off something; not affected by something

> This looks like a serious case of **strep** to me.

strep
(strep) a common bacteria that can cause infection and illness, including strep throat. It's short for *Streptococcus*. In severe cases, it can get inside the skin and cause "flesh-eating disease."

Say What?

Here's some other lingo a specialist might use on the job.

ER
(EE-ahr) an area in a hospital for patients who need immediate attention; it's short for *emergency room*.
"Get her to the **ER** now, before she loses too much blood."

ICU
(eye-SEE-yoo) an area in a hospital where very ill patients stay; it's short for *intensive care unit*.
"He needs to stay in the **ICU** until he can breathe on his own."

IV
(EYE-vee) a device for giving medication or fluids through a vein; it's short for *intravenous*.
"She needs antibiotics quickly. Hook her up to an **IV**."

OR
(OH-ahr) an area in a hospital where surgeries are performed; it's short for *operating room*.
"We'll need her in the **OR** for surgery tomorrow at nine."

9

CELLULITIS ▶

SYMPTOMS Usually caused by staph, it's a swelling of the skin and tissues underneath. It usually forms on the upper body, arms, or legs. Skin turns painful, red, and tender. Swelling can blister and turn into a scab.

TREATMENT Oral or IV antibiotics

A Rash of Problems

What happens when bacteria gets under your skin?

Bacteria are tiny, single-celled life-forms. They outnumber all other living things on earth. There are billions of bacteria all around you. They live in the water and the earth. They're in the air and inside your own body.

Most bacteria are perfectly harmless. Others can make you sick. Staph and strep are two of the most common disease-causing bacteria. If they get in your mouth or lungs, they can cause diseases like strep throat or **pneumonia**. When they get under the skin, things can get nasty. What are the telltale signs of a staph or strep infection? It's not pretty, but take a look.

NECROTIZING FASCIITIS ▶

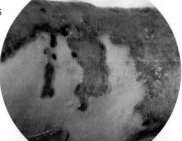

SYMPTOMS Severe infection that destroys skin and soft tissue. It's caused by a rare kind of strep bacterium. It can be fatal.

TREATMENT Immediate hospitalization; antibiotics to kill the bacteria; surgery to cut out infected and dead tissue

IMPETIGO ▼

SYMPTOMS A staph or strep infection that causes pimple-like sores around the nose and mouth. The blisters can burst, ooze, and then form a thick crust. The infection can itch and spread.

TREATMENT Ointment or antibiotics

FOLLICULITIS ▲

SYMPTOMS Tiny white-headed pimples, often caused by staph. They form on the scalp, at the base of hair shafts. They are often found on girls who wear their hair tightly pulled back.

TREATMENT It usually clears in one week.

BOILS ▶

SYMPTOMS Swollen red sores filled with pus, usually caused by staph. They are found especially in the armpits and the groin area.

TREATMENT Warm-water soaks. In some cases, **boils** may need to be operated on and drained of pus.

SCALDED SKIN SYNDROME ▼

SYMPTOMS Staph infection that turns into a rash and then causes the skin to peel off. Affects children under age five.

TREATMENT Ointment

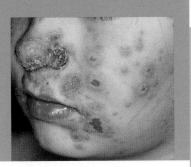

◀SCARLET FEVER

SYMPTOMS Rash made up of tiny red pinpoints. Can follow a case of strep throat. It begins as a red rash on the sides of the chest and stomach. It may spread around the body.

TREATMENT Antibiotics

The Medical Team

It takes more than one doctor to handle a bacterial infection. Here's a look at some of the experts who make up the infectious disease team.

CLINICAL PATHOLOGISTS
They examine blood and other body fluids under micoscopes for evidence of infection.

NEUROLOGISTS
When a case involves an infection of the brain and nerves, they identify the damage and help manage the care of the patient.

INFECTIOUS DISEASE DOCTORS
They specialize in diseases caused by bacteria and/or viruses.

INTERNAL MEDICINE DOCTORS
When a case involves an infection of internal organs, they identify the problem and start the antibiotic treatment.

CRITICAL CARE DOCTORS
They treat patients in the ICU. They are usually experts in the lungs and may manage ventilators, which help patients breathe.

NEPHROLOGISTS
They specialize in diseases of the kidneys. The kidneys filter waste and can be affected by bacterial infections.

INTENSIVE CARE NURSES
They provide 24-hour care to patients in the intensive care unit (ICU).

TRUE-LIFE
CASE FILES!

24 hours a day, 7 days a week, 365 days a year, infectious disease specialists fight to keep patients healthy.

IN THIS SECTION:

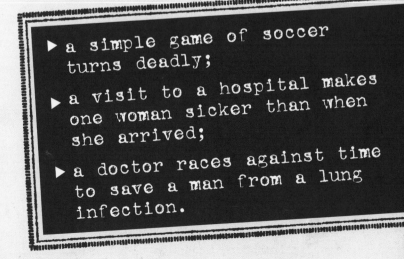

- a simple game of soccer turns deadly;

- a visit to a hospital makes one woman sicker than when she arrived;

- a doctor races against time to save a man from a lung infection.

How do infectious disease specialists get the job done?

Each of the cases you're about to read is very different. But the steps the doctors followed are similar. Doctors use a scientific process to figure out, or diagnose, what's wrong with a patient. You can follow this process as you read the case studies. Keep an eye out for the icons below.

THE QUESTION At the beginning of each case, the doctors ask **one or two main questions** about their patients.

THE EVIDENCE The next step is to **gather and analyze evidence**. Doctors examine a patient. They look for symptoms. They run tests. Then they analyze the evidence to figure out what it means.

THE CONCLUSION Along the way, doctors come up with theories about what may be wrong. They test these theories in the lab. They also compare them to a patient's symptoms. Do the results back up the theory? **If so, they've reached a diagnosis, or conclusion**.

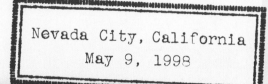
Nevada City, California
May 9, 1998

The Terrible Tale of the Flesh-Eating Disease

A minor injury from a soccer game turns into a deadly infection. Can a doctor stop the bacteria before they kill their host?

Spiked!

It's just a minor sports injury—isn't it?

On Saturday mornings, Bo Salisbury played indoor soccer with teens from his church. Salisbury was a 50-year-old postmaster in Nevada City, California. He usually played goalie. But he liked to show the kids that he still had some smooth moves left from his high school playing days.

Salisbury was in goal on May 9, 1998. It was a normal Saturday. He had a cold, but that wasn't going to slow him down. At one point, players crowded into the box, fighting for the ball. Salisbury blocked a shot, but the shooter's follow-through hit his left ankle. Salisbury limped off the field with a stinging bruise.

In May 1998, Bo Salisbury got a bruise on his ankle during his weekly soccer game. Would this injury sideline him—for good?

The next day, the pain was worse. Salisbury took some aspirin and went to lunch at a Chinese restaurant. By 2 P.M., his ankle was killing him.

Salisbury went to the emergency room at a nearby hospital. A doctor examined the bruise, which was turning red. He decided it was just a nasty sports injury. The doctor gave Salisbury some painkillers and sent him home.

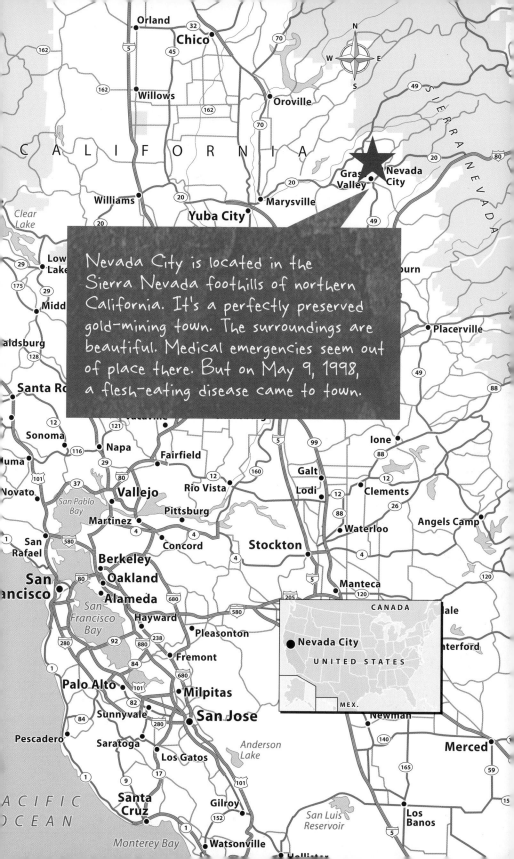

Nevada City is located in the Sierra Nevada foothills of northern California. It's a perfectly preserved gold-mining town. The surroundings are beautiful. Medical emergencies seem out of place there. But on May 9, 1998, a flesh-eating disease came to town.

By Monday morning, Salisbury was in terrible pain. He was **nauseated** and sweating. His leg throbbed. He went to see his doctor, who sent him straight to the hospital. He told the doctors there that he felt like he was dying.

Rapid Decline

Bo Salisbury is failing fast—and doctors can't explain why.

This time, it was clear that Bo Salisbury had more than a sports injury. But what was causing the other symptoms? The doctors needed a **diagnosis**—and fast.

They took Salisbury's blood pressure. It was dropping quickly. They examined his leg. A blue-gray bruise had begun to spread out from the ankle. Doctors took a **blood sample** to test for a bacterial infection. While they waited for the results, they gave Salisbury an antibiotic.

Meanwhile, Salisbury got worse. He began to slip in and out of consciousness. He

Bad weather made travel by helicopter impossible. So Salisbury was taken by ambulance to the University of California, Davis Medical Center.

prepared himself to die. He told his teenage daughter not to cry. He even made her promise to study for her final exams. "There's nothing anyone can do for me now," he said.

Salisbury's doctors didn't know what to do. But they knew someone who might.

The weather was too stormy for a helicopter, so hospital orderlies wheeled Salisbury into an ambulance. It raced through the streets on its way to the University of California, Davis Medical Center. Meanwhile, the mysterious bruise continued to creep up his leg.

Last Chance

Dr. Susan Murin takes the case. Can she figure out what's killing Salisbury?

At UC Davis, Salisbury was met by Dr. Susan Murin. She heads a team of doctors at the intensive care unit (ICU) there. That's the part of the hospital that treats the sickest patients. When they arrive, most of Dr. Murin's patients are close to death. Four out of five of them walk out alive.

"Working in the ICU is never boring," says Dr. Murin, a 44-year-old mother of three. "You see everything down here. You're more than a specialist. You have to be able to treat everything. You never know who is going to come through that door."

Minutes after Salisbury arrived, Dr. Murin had a team of doctors at his bedside. She worked with infectious disease specialist Dr. Jeff Jones. The team gave Salisbury oxygen and fluids. He could still talk, but he was failing fast.

Salisbury was a tricky case, even for Dr. Murin and Dr. Jones. Salisbury had kept in great shape. He had no history of illness. In two days he had gone from perfect health to the verge of death. What was wrong?

Dr. Murin looked at Salisbury's leg. The purplish bruise was spreading slowly up the leg. To Dr. Murin, it looked like "rotten meat." The flesh had gone cold. A normal infection would be red and warm. This leg wasn't getting blood. That led her to believe that Salisbury had a blood clot. The clot was keeping blood from flowing to his leg.

Dr. Susan Murin heads a team of doctors in the ICU at the UC Davis Medical Center. She had to act quickly to save Salisbury's life.

Bo Salisbury's blood culture tested positive for the dangerous strep bacteria.

Dr. Murin ordered an **ultrasound**. This device uses sound waves to create a picture of the inside of the leg. The image showed no blood clot.

Just then a call came from the other hospital. Salisbury's blood test results were in. They showed traces of a bacterium called *Streptococcus pyrogenes*.

Murin had her diagnosis. Inside Salisbury's body, the infection was causing his flesh to die.

UNDER THE MICROSCOPE

How do doctors test for infections?

In both staph and strep cases, bacteria have invaded a person's body. Here's how doctors fight it.

Step one: The Tests

blood test: to find out if the body is fighting an infection. If it is, the person's white blood cell count could be high.

urine test: to find out if the patient's kidneys are working well and whether they are getting enough fluids. Often, infections will cause a person to become dehydrated.

pus culture: the lab will actually grow bacteria from this sample to test it and find out what is infecting the patient.

Step two: The Treatment

Most staph and strep infections can be treated with antibiotics. Serious cases may require surgery to remove the infected areas.

21

Flesh Eaters

Sometimes, relatively harmless bacteria can turn into a gruesome killer.

Necrotizing fasciitis on a human leg. At first Salisbury thought he had a bruise. Then it started spreading up his leg.

The test results proved to Dr. Murin and Dr. Jones that Salisbury had necrotizing fasciitis (NF). It's a disease caused by the strep bacteria. As many as 15 to 30 percent of people carry strep in their bodies. Most have no symptoms at all. But they can pass the bacteria to others. Salisbury probably got it through the bruise on his ankle.

In most people, strep is relatively harmless. It causes strep throat or impetigo. Those diseases are easily cured with antibiotics. In extremely rare cases, strep turns into NF, which is far more deadly. Only 500 to 1,500 Americans get it every year. More than one in five of them die from it.

Dr. Murin had seen NF only once before. But she knew how it kills. The bacteria produce toxins—poisons—in a patient's body. The toxins kill the soft tissue, or fascia, below the skin. It spreads fast, killing tissue as it goes. If left untreated, NF patients die.

Salisbury was already close. The antibiotics weren't working. His blood pressure kept dropping. He needed more and more oxygen. Dr. Murin was in a race against time.

"This thing travels fast," Salisbury says. "In 72 hours, you kill it—or it kills you."

ANTIBIOTIC ATTACK

An accident led to the creation of a wonder drug.

When bacteria strikes and causes infection, humans turn to antibiotics.

Professor Alexander Fleming, a research scientist in London, England, discovered antibiotics in 1928. He was researching staph infections and growing **cultures** in petri dishes. Professor Fleming went on vacation and left one dish out in the open.

A Killer Mold

When Fleming returned, he noticed the bacteria had multiplied, forming colonies. Curiously, he noticed a funny, green mold sitting at one edge. Around it, all the bacteria had died.

Somehow the mold was killing bacteria. Professor Fleming studied the mold and saw tiny drops of fluid on it. He removed the fluid and found that it could kill germs in a test tube. He called this **penicillin**. It became the first antibiotic used to treat disease.

Today, antibiotics are made in labs. Researchers are always working to develop new ones to fight new kinds of bacteria.

The Race

Can a team of surgeons stop the bacteria before it kills the patient?

Dr. Murin called a famous surgeon. She pleaded with him to get Salisbury into his operating room—fast!

Two hours after his ambulance roared into the UC Davis parking lot, Salisbury was in surgery. Even so, Dr. Murin thought Salisbury's chances were poor. "I honestly thought he wasn't going to make it," she says. "He's such a nice guy. I was pulling for him. At the very least, I thought they'd have to amputate his leg."

Using special drugs, doctors put Salisbury into a **coma**. That way, his body could handle the shock of what was next.

Surgeons raced the bacteria as it marched up Salisbury's leg. They cut into the skin and began to slice off the infected tissue. In some places on his leg, they had to cut all the way down to the bone.

Finally, they were sure they had all of the bacteria. They'd had to remove most of the flesh from Salisbury's toe to his hip. But when he left the operating room, Salisbury still had his leg—and his life.

Recovery

For Bo Salisbury, surviving necrotizing fasciitis was just the first step.

Salisbury woke up ten days later. Doctors had spent a week replacing the flesh on his leg through skin grafts. They peeled flesh from other parts of Salisbury's body. Then they sewed it onto the leg. Salisbury felt like he had been skinned alive. "I'm all striped now," he jokes. "People stare at me when I wear shorts."

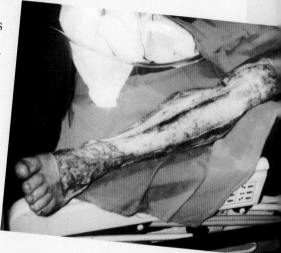

Bo Salisbury's leg after the surgeries. To get rid of necrotizing fasciitis, all of the infected tissue must be removed. Then the doctors have to get rid of any bacteria before new skin is grafted on.

In all, Salisbury underwent eight skin grafts. The treatments left him weak and depressed.

Little by little, Salisbury recovered. He started rehab to strengthen his body and learn to do everyday activities. His first workout was simply to sit up for ten minutes at a time. After five months, Salisbury was finally able to leave the hospital and go home.

Today, Salisbury runs three miles (4.8 km) a day. He even competed in a five-kilometer race. Some Saturdays, you can still find him playing goalie for his church soccer team.

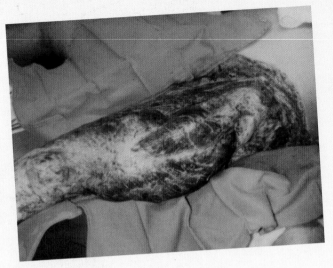

Salisbury's leg after the operation. His entire body was swollen. That's because his organs had failed, and his body was retaining fluids.

Bo Salisbury sometimes wonders how he got such a rare disease. Why him, after all? Strep has no effect on some people, while it almost kills others. Even Dr. Murin can't explain exactly why. "There are so many mysteries in medicine that we still don't understand," she says.

Dr. Murin believes Salisbury's survival was part luck and part good teamwork. "He got the exact care he needed, as quickly as possible," she says. "When you see it all come together like that to save a person's life, well, it's the most joyous feeling a doctor can have." 24/7

Strep found its way into Bo Salisbury's body on the soccer field. In the next case, the infection came from a favorite breeding ground for bacteria—the hospital.

Los Angeles County
Medical Center
Los Angeles, California
August 23, 2004

No Time to Lose

A woman survives surgery—but gets a terrible infection. She'll need emergency surgery to save her life.

Names and other details have been changed
to protect patient confidentiality.

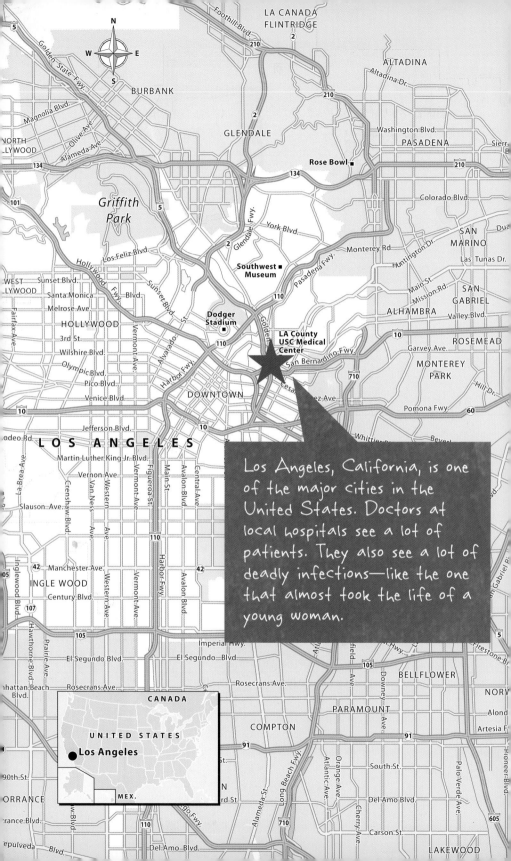

N
W E
S

Golden State Fwy.
Foothill Blvd.

LA CANADA
FLINTRIDGE

ALTADINA
Altadina Dr.

BURBANK

Magnolia Blvd.

Olive Ave.

Alameda Ave.

GLENDALE

Washington Blvd.
PASADENA
Sierr.
B

NORTH
LYWOOD

Rose Bowl ■

Colorado Blvd.

Griffith
Park

Glendale Fwy.
York Blvd.

SAN
MARINO
Dua

Monterey Rd.
Las Tunas Dr.

WEST
LYWOOD

Hollywood Fwy.

Los Feliz Blvd.

Sunset Blvd.

Sunset Blvd.

Santa Monica Blvd.

Melrose Ave.

Southwest ■
Museum

Pasadena Fwy.

Huntington Dr.

Main St.

Mission Rd.

SAN
GABRIEL

Fairfax Ave.

HOLLYWOOD

3rd St.

Wilshire Blvd.

Olympic Blvd.

Pico Blvd.

Venice Blvd.

Vermont Ave.

Alvarado

Harbor Fwy.

Dodger
Stadium
■

LA County
USC Medical
Center

San Bernardino Fwy.

ALHAMBRA

Valley Blvd.

ROSEMEAD

Garvey Ave.

MONTEREY
PARK

Cesar ez Ave.

Pomona Fwy.

Hill Dr.

odeo Rd.

LOS ANGELES

Jefferson Blvd.

Martin Luther King Jr. Blvd.

Vernon Ave.

Slauson Ave.

Figueroa St.

Main St.

Avalon Blvd.

Central Ave.

Whittier

Bever

Los Angeles, California, is one
of the major cities in the
United States. Doctors at
local hospitals see a lot of
patients. They also see a lot of
deadly infections—like the one
that almost took the life of a
young woman.

La Brea Ave.

Crenshaw Blvd.

Western Ave.

Van Ness Ave.

Manchester Ave.

INGLE WOOD

Century Blvd.

Harbor Fwy.

Avalon Blvd.

Vermont Ave.

Western Ave.

Imperial Hwy.

El Segundo Blvd.

El Segundo Blvd.

field

Hwy.

BELLFLOWER

NORV

Alond

Hawthorne Blvd.

Prairie Ave.

hattan Beach
Blvd.

Rosecrans Ave.

Rosecrans Ave.

Downey

Ave.

PARAMOUNT

COMPTON

Artesia

CANADA

UNITED STATES
● Los Angeles

MEX.

St.

Long Beach Fwy.

Alameda St.

Orange Ave.

Atlantic Ave.

South St.

Cherry Ave.

Del Amo Blvd.

Palo Verde Ave.

Pioneer Blvd.

epulveda Blvd.

Del Amo Blvd.

Carson St.

LAKEWOOD

Home at Last

Rita DaSilva has just had surgery. And she's ready to get back to her life.

In August 2004, Rita DaSilva was happy to be home from the hospital. She had just had surgery on her gallbladder. Now she could get back to her busy life. DaSilva had five kids, ages seven to 14. She worked as a Los Angeles city bus driver. She couldn't afford to be sick for long.

But DaSilva couldn't ignore the way she felt. She had a fever. And she wasn't healing well from the surgery. The doctors had made four small **incisions** in her stomach. One of the wounds was red and swollen. The skin around it was warm to the touch and very sore. DaSilva had already missed a follow-up appointment at the hospital. Now she couldn't wait any longer.

After two weeks at home, DaSilva went to the Los Angeles County Clinic. A doctor there examined her incisions. The skin had healed. But the redness, the swelling, and the warmth were signs of danger. It looked like the wound had become infected.

The doctor ordered DaSilva to the hospital for tests to find out if she had an infection. If she did, they needed to know right away.

This incision is red and swollen with pus. Like Rita DaSilva's incision, this one became infected after surgery.

DaSilva didn't want to go. "I can't take any more time for this," she said. "My kids need me, and I'm afraid I'll get fired."

The doctor told her gently but firmly that she needed to go. If she didn't, her kids could be left without a mother.

CT scans are used to get images of a patient's body tissues and organs. Doctors ran a CT scan on DaSilva to see how deep the infection was.

Staph Strikes

There are bacteria growing in DaSilva's wound. How deep is the infection?

THE EVIDENCE

At the hospital, a nurse got to work right away. She took a blood sample and a urine sample from DaSilva. She sent them both to the lab. Tests would show whether DaSilva had a bacterial infection.

DaSilva then had a **CT scan**. A CT scan uses x-rays to look inside the body. If the wound were infected, the scan would show how deep the infection went.

While the lab technicians worked, DaSilva waited in a hospital bed. Before long, she got a visit from

Dr. Tiffany Grunwald. Dr. Grunwald had been a part of the team that operated on DaSilva's gallbladder.

Dr. Grunwald told DaSilva the news. The tests showed she had a staph infection. *Staphylococcus aureus* bacteria were feeding on the flesh in her wound.

If a staph infection is discovered early, it can be treated with antibiotics. If not, the bacteria grow under the skin. They spread out, looking for more flesh to eat. Dead tissue and pus are left at the center of the infected area.

Dr. Grunwald told DaSilva that her staph infection had not been caught early enough. Antibiotics would no longer help. DaSilva needed surgery to remove the infected tissue.

"I don't have time for more surgery," DaSilva protested. But Dr. Grunwald promised her she would be out by the end of the day.

DaSilva had no choice. She agreed to have the surgery. Nurses began preparing her for the operating room.

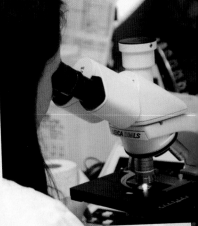

DaSilva's lab tests showed that she had a serious staph infection.

HOSPITAL STAPH

Here's why the place you go to be cured can also make you sick.

Staph is the most feared bacterial organism for a reason. Every time the bacteria encounter an antibiotic, the weak strains die. But some of the bacteria may mutate (or change) to a type resistant to the antibiotics. Those bacteria survive the antibiotics and can reproduce.

Super-Staph

One of the main breeding grounds for these persistent bacteria are hospitals. About 500,000 patients a year get staph infections in health-care facilities. Nearly 100,000 of them die.

Hospitals do everything they can to kill bacteria. Health-care workers wear gloves and face masks to keep from spreading germs. They wash often with warm water and soap. They keep their equipment perfectly clean.

Still, no matter how clean a hospital is, it can't keep up with the bacteria. Sick patients come in by the dozens. Each patient brings more bacteria. The tiny germs find places to hide. They live on the walls and in the air, just waiting to find a victim.

A Supply of Victims

Hospitals also have plenty of victims. Many patients are old or sick. Their **immune systems** are weak. The body's immune system protects it against disease. Healthy ones do a good job of fighting off staph infections. Weak ones make the body an easy target.

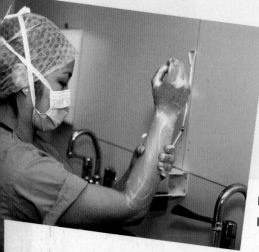

Health-care workers take precautions to protect themselves and their patients.

Under the Knife

DaSilva has a serious infection. Doctors rush her to the OR.

In a matter of hours, DaSilva was in the OR. A doctor gave her **anesthesia**. Within seconds she was asleep.

Dr. Grunwald performed the surgery. She made a small cut above the infected incision. The infection had spread deeper than she expected. She drained about two ounces (60 ml) of pus from the wound. Then she carefully cut out the dead tissue.

Dr. Grunwald stopped when she had removed all the infected tissue. A nurse cleaned the wound with an antibiotic soap.

When the wound was clean, the doctors left it open. They packed it with soft gauze. "Bacteria love dark, closed environments," Dr. Grunwald explains. Exposing the wound to the air would make it easier to clean. All bacteria would die.

Dr. Tiffany Grunwald is a surgeon in Los Angeles. When she saw DaSilva's infection, she ordered her patient to the OR.

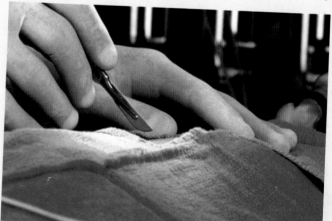

Rita DaSilva had to have surgery to remove the infected tissue around her incision.

Home at Last

DaSilva is allowed to go home, but her recovery continues.

Before DaSilva was released from the hospital, the doctor instructed her how to change the gauze in her wound.

DaSilva woke up feeling sore. She was sick to her stomach from the anesthesia. But she was determined to go home.

But first, Dr. Grunwald spoke with her. The doctor reminded DaSilva to come back in a week. Then Dr. Grunwald showed her patient how to take care of the wound. DaSilva had to insert small strips of gauze inside the wound. Then, twice a day, she had to remove the gauze and replace it with fresh strips.

This process would keep the wound from becoming infected. First, changing the gauze would help remove leftover dead tissue. Second, the gauze would prevent the wound from closing up. There were still bacteria in the wound. And if the wound closed too soon, it would have a dark, warm place to grow.

DaSilva went home and followed the doctor's orders. She was happy to have her life back and eager to follow the doctor's instructions—and stay out of the hospital. **24/7**

Bacteria entered Rita DaSilva's body through a surgical incision. What happens when staph gets into the lungs?

Kaiser Medical Center
Woodland Hills, California
December 26, 2005

Help! I Can't Breathe!

It seemed like just a bad case of the flu. So why is the patient now fighting for his life?

Names and other details have been changed to protect patient confidentiality.

He's Collapsed!

In a crowded waiting room, Henry Johns starts gasping for air.

The emergency room at Kaiser Medical Center in Woodland Hills, California, was crowded with sick people. The city had more flu cases than it could handle.

Henry Johns sat with the crowd in the waiting room. He had gotten the flu before. But it had never made him this sick. He was sweating and he could barely speak. Soon, he started coughing up blood.

The front desk nurse noticed Johns in pain. Within minutes, he was moved to the top of the waiting list. Nurses put him on a rolling bed. They wheeled him in to see an ER doctor.

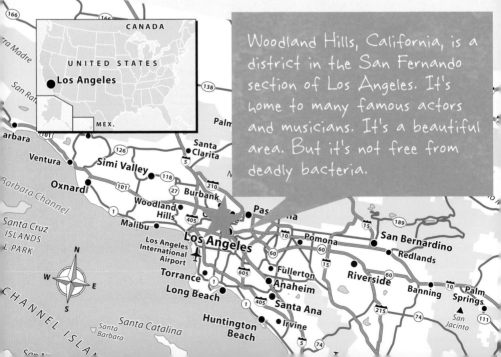

Woodland Hills, California, is a district in the San Fernando section of Los Angeles. It's home to many famous actors and musicians. It's a beautiful area. But it's not free from deadly bacteria.

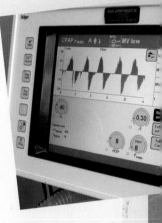

Henry Johns was diagnosed with pneumonia, an infection of the lungs. In this photograph, the patient's left lung is infected with pneumonia.

The doctor listened to Johns's lungs. Johns breathed in rattling gasps. The doctor knew the sound right away. Johns had pneumonia—and it sounded like a bad case. Pneumonia causes the lungs to swell and fill with fluid. Patients have trouble breathing. Eventually, they can die from respiratory failure.

At this point, Johns's lungs were so swollen he couldn't breathe. The ER doctor placed a tube into Johns's mouth and pushed it down his airway. The tube was hooked up to a ventilator machine, which pumped air into Johns's lungs. Without the machine, Johns would die.

The patient was safe for the moment. But he needed immediate attention. Pneumonia can be caused by bacteria, viruses, or other organisms. Doctors need to understand the cause so they know how to treat the disease.

What had caused Johns's pneumonia?

Nurses transferred Johns to the ICU of the hospital for tests.

Johns's breathing was monitored by a machine like this one.

THE QUESTION
?

The Race Begins

Doctors run tests on Johns. But they can't afford to wait for the results.

Dr. Pamela Nagami was waiting for Johns in the ICU. She is an infectious disease specialist. The minute she saw Johns, she knew she had to move quickly.

THE EVIDENCE

Dr. Nagami ordered a series of tests.

First, the critical care nurse pushed a thin plastic tube down Johns's airway. She sucked out a small amount of fluid from his lungs. Then, the nurse took a blood sample from his arm. These two samples should reveal what caused the pneumonia.

Next, another doctor took a sample of spinal fluid from Johns's lower back. Dr. Nagami wanted to test for a disease called **meningitis**. Meningitis is an infection that affects the brain and the nerves.

But Dr. Nagami had to act before the test results came back. She thought that Johns might have a staph infection. Staph bacteria can cause a disease called cavitary pneumonia. Cavitary pneumonia destroys lung tissue. If that's what Johns had, the bacteria were tearing holes in his lungs.

Johns needed medication—now.

A critical care nurse took a blood sample from Johns for testing. This blood sample would show what had caused his pneumonia.

INSIDE THE LAB

Here's how doctors track down a staph infection.

How do doctors know when a patient has a staph infection? First, they take a sample of blood, urine, pus from a skin infection, or fluid from the lungs. They send the sample to a lab.

Name That Bacteria

At the lab, technicians try to get the bacteria in the sample to grow. They store it at body temperature. They give it nutrients.

When they have enough bacteria, they add chemicals that will identify the bacteria. They can also look at the sample under a microscope. Staph bacteria look like a cluster of grapes and appear in large, round golden-yellow colonies.

Kill That Bacteria

Next, the technicians test to see what kind of medicine will kill the bacteria. They drip the antibiotics—one at a time—onto the bacteria. If the bacteria die, they've found the right medicine.

A lab technician looks for MRSA—a form of staph bacteria—under a microscope.

Attacking the Superbug

Johns needs treatment right away. But what exactly are the doctors treating?

Dr. Nagami knew she had to get Johns on antibiotics. But she couldn't be sure which kind to give him. Each antibiotic is designed to kill certain bacteria. Without the test

A close-up of MRSA in a petri dish. MRSA is a strain of staph that's resistant to certain antibiotics. Over the years, certain bacteria have become more resistant to traditional medicines and are harder to kill.

results, Dr. Nagami didn't know which bacteria were in Johns's lungs.

This case was tricky. Normally, doctors use antibiotics in the penicillin family to fight staph infections. But some staph bacteria no longer respond to these antibiotics. These bacteria are sometimes called "superbugs" because they are resistant to antibiotics that worked well years ago.

Dr. Nagami thought Johns could have the superbug. So, she gave him vancomycin. Doctors call vancomycin "the last resort drug." They try to use it only if other antibiotics fail. In this case, Dr. Nagami didn't have time to try anything else. Hours after checking into the hospital, Johns was already down to his last chance.

CHASING THE BUG

If antibiotics don't kill bacteria, they make the germ stronger.

Antibiotics have saved millions of lives. But the bacteria are fighting back. And they get more resistant with every battle.

Antibiotics work by killing off weak bacteria. But in every infection, there may be a few bacteria that survive. With the weak bacteria dead, the stronger bacteria have room to grow and reproduce.

Over time, these new, stronger superbugs may become resistant to antibiotics.

Stopping the Superbugs

How do we keep the superbugs from taking over? Experts say doctors need to stop prescribing antibiotics unless they know the patient has an infection.

Often, doctors prescribe antibiotics for colds, sore throats, and earaches—just in case the patient has an infection.

However, most of the time, these minor health problems are caused by *viruses*. And antibiotics don't even work on viruses!

So if the patient *doesn't* have an infection, the doctor is helping strong bacteria grow. The weak bacteria are killed off, giving the stronger ones room to grow. And the next time the patient *really* needs an antibiotic, those strong bacteria are ready to fight it off.

Results Are In

Johns has the right medicine—but he's still fighting for his life.

Johns lay in his hospital bed and waited for the test results. He didn't look good. An air tube pumped oxygen into his lungs. An

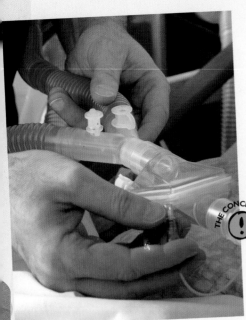

Because of the staph infection, Johns couldn't breathe on his own. A ventilator had to do that for him while his body fought the pneumonia.

IV (intravenous) tube dripped fluids and medicine into a vein in his arm.

THE CONCLUSION Then the test results came in. One by one, the lab technicians called the ICU. The spinal fluid test came back negative. Johns did not have meningitis. The fluid from his lungs, however, showed that Dr. Nagami was right. Johns had the superbug.

Everyone in the ICU was relieved. Johns already had the right medicine in his body. Vancomycin had been dripping into his bloodstream for hours.

Still, Johns was in critical condition. He wasn't breathing on his own. And the infection had spread beyond the lungs. Bacteria had damaged his kidneys. Normally, the kidneys filter poisons out of the body. But Johns's kidneys weren't doing their job. His body was poisoning itself from the inside out.

A kidney specialist examined Johns. He used a tube called a **catheter** to help clear out the poisons in Johns's body. Then everyone waited for the antibiotic to do its work.

Back from the Edge

Little by little, Johns begins to improve.

After eight days in intensive care, Johns was finally out of danger. The antibiotic had killed off the bacteria in his lungs. He no longer needed the breathing tube. His kidneys began to work again. He didn't need a catheter. He was weak, but he could sit up.

Johns was wheeled out of the ICU—but the work wasn't done yet. He had barely moved for more than a week. He needed a physical therapist to help him rebuild his strength. He also needed a respiratory therapist. He began doing breathing exercises to strengthen his lungs.

After Henry Johns left the ICU, he had to regain strength in his muscles and lungs.

Finally, after a month in the hospital, Johns went home.

Dr. Nagami was left to wonder at the power of a tiny germ.

Staph has always had the potential to kill. It can get into the lungs and the bloodstream. It can cause pneumonia and leave people gasping for breath. It can damage other organs, such as the kidneys.

But in Dr. Nagami's opinion, staph infections are getting worse. In the past, she says, staph often just caused small red sores on the skin. Patients would go to the doctor to get the pus drained from the sore. Then they'd go home.

But now there seem to be more super-staph infections that are resistant to antibiotics.

Henry Johns was lucky, Dr. Nagami reflects. He got the right medicine at the right time. Without it, he would have been in trouble. "Had we waited until the lab tests came back," Dr. Nagami said, "Henry would have died." 24/7

Staph bacteria as seen through a microscope. Staph is known for its grape-like clusters. This deadly bacteria can get into a person's lungs and cause pneumonia.

MEDICAL DOWNLOAD

Here's some more infectious stuff about bacteria for your reading pleasure.

IN THIS SECTION:

- ▶ where germs have popped up in the past;
- ▶ infectious diseases in the news;
- ▶ the tools that are used to study germs;
- ▶ whether being an infectious disease doctor might be in your future!

3500—1500 B.C.
Good Molds
Many cultures use molds as medicine. South American Indians wear moldy sandals to fight foot infection. The Egyptians and Chinese use mold to treat rashes and wounds.

1300s The Plague
The bubonic plague infects most of Europe. It was a bacterial disease spread by rats. The bacteria could kill within a few days. It killed between 20 and 30 million people.

Key Dates in the History

Humans have been battling bacteria for thousands of years.

1928—29 Antibiotics Are Born
Scottish scientist Alexander Fleming (*right*) discovers penicillin. It is the first modern antibiotic. It takes more than ten years to produce it in large quantities. During World War II (1939–1945), it is used to treat thousands of wounded soldiers.

1870 Pasteur's Discovery

French scientist Louis Pasteur (*right*) discovers that bacteria cause wine and milk to go sour. His work leads to the germ theory of disease. The germ theory states that many diseases are caused by bacteria. Those diseases can spread from person to person as bacteria are passed around.

Late 1890s Cleaning Up

Doctors begin using sterilization to kill bacteria. They heat instruments and wash hands with soap. They also wear masks and gowns to avoid spreading bacteria.

of Infection

1950s and 1960s New Drugs

Researchers develop new drugs to fight staph. Methicillin, oxacillin, and vancomycin are the most effective.

Today New Superbugs

Staph begins to resist treatment with vancomycin. Experts say we need another big medical discovery to stay one step ahead of the bacteria.

Do Millions Have the Superbug?

December 2005

A superbug could be hiding in your nose. Don't laugh. A new study shows that about two million Americans carry a form of bacteria that is very hard to treat. The study was done by the Centers for Disease Control and Prevention (CDC) in Atlanta, Georgia.

Researchers took samples from the noses of 10,000 people. One-third of the samples were infected with staph bacteria. Nearly one percent of those samples had MRSA. MRSA is a form of staph that does not respond as well to some antibiotics.

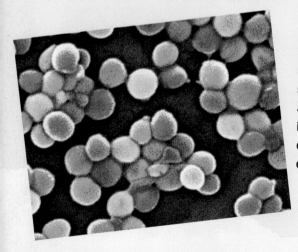

This is MRSA bacteria, as seen under a colored scanning electron micrograph. MRSA stands for Methicillin-resistant *Staphylococcus aureus*. MRSA is carried by 30 percent of the population without causing any symptoms.

To combat the deadly MRSA bacteria, the locker room of the Washington Redskins football team had to be thoroughly cleaned.

Staph Putting Athletes on Disabled List

November 2006

They call it the superbug. MRSA is a strain of staph that is resistant to many antibiotics. After it was discovered in 1971, most MRSA victims got the super-strong bacteria in the hospital.

But these days, MRSA is creeping out into the world. One common place for MRSA is locker rooms and gyms. MRSA has also been found on artificial grass playing fields.

Since 2003, three NFL football teams have had outbreaks. The Washington Redskins even had to have the entire locker room sterilized.

What's another new MRSA destination? The superbug is also showing up at tattoo parlors.

The War on Germs

Have a look at some of the tools and equipment used by health-care workers.

syringe and needle
Nurses use a syringe and needle to inject medicine into patients. They're also used to withdraw fluid from the body. Push down on the syringe and it injects. Pull up and it withdraws fluid.

microscope Lab techs use it to look for bacteria in fluid samples taken from patients.

petri dishes Lab techs store fluid samples in these dishes. They keep them at body temperature so the bacteria will grow.

slide This is a thin piece of glass with smears of the sample. A slide goes right under the lens of a microscope.

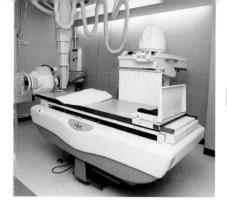

x-ray machine These machines take pictures of the inside of the body. They can show damage that an infection has done to tissue and bone.

CT scanner A CT scanner creates a three-dimensional x-ray of the inside of the body. CT stands for *computed topography*.

MRI This device uses radio waves to take highly detailed pictures of a patient's body. It creates a computer image. MRI stands for *magnetic resonance imaging*.

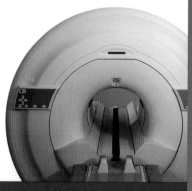

UNIVERSAL PRECAUTIONS

All health-care workers follow a set of rules called universal precautions when dealing with the blood or body fluids of people with infections. Universal precautions include:

▶ using only sterilized, disposable needles and syringes
▶ immediately throwing away needles in a safe container
▶ washing hands with soap and water before and after working with patients
▶ using protective barriers such as gloves, gowns, aprons, masks, and goggles for direct contact with blood and other body fluids
▶ disinfecting instruments and other equipment

HELP WANTED:
Infectious Disease Specialist

Are you interested in studying infectious diseases? Here's more information about the field.

Q&A: DR. REKHA MURTHY

24/7: What kind of training did you have?

Dr. Rekha Murthy is a clinical professor of medicine at UCLA and an infectious disease specialist at Cedars-Sinai Hospital in Los Angeles.

DR. REKHA MURTHY: After I graduated from college, I went to medical school. Then I worked three years as a resident in internal medicine.

24/7: What got you interested in infectious diseases?

MURTHY: I got very interested in fields likes cancer and infectious disease because you have to know a lot about all the body systems. I also loved the detective work that infectious disease often requires.

24/7: Describe a typical day at your job.

MURTHY: I usually start at 8 A.M. I begin by seeing patients. Other doctors ask for my advice on cases concerning infection and fever. I help identify the disease. I guide the medical team on tests to order, treatment, and antibiotic recommendations. I give on-the-job training to doctors, medical students, nurses, and staff. I also do research and work with trainees. Typically my day ends around 5 or 6 P.M., but I carry a beeper 24/7.

24/7: What happens after work?

MURTHY: I bring medical journals home and look up information online. I network with colleagues to discuss complicated cases. Medicine moves so fast, especially in my field. We have to get the information as quickly as possible and be a resource to the other staff in the hospital.

24/7: What do you like most about your work?

MURTHY: I like that it's never the same. I always feel like I'm learning. And I really feel like I am making a difference by sharing information and participating with patient care.

24/7: What do you like least about your work?

MURTHY: When patients die, you can get overwhelmed by the sadness of it. You ask, What could I have done differently? But sometimes, even with the best treatment, you can't change the outcome.

24/7: What advice do you have for young people who are interested in this field?

MURTHY: Develop good interpersonal skills. You need to communicate with patients in a compassionate manner. You also need to be able to be seen as a leader. You need to move quickly to solve problems.

THE STATS

DAY JOB: Most infectious disease doctors work as primary-care physicians.

MONEY: The average salary for an infectious disease doctor is $185,920.

EDUCATION: Infectious disease doctors must finish the following.
▶ 4 years of college
▶ 4 years of medical school
▶ 3 or more years training as a doctor
▶ 2–3 years of specialized training in infectious diseases

THE NUMBERS: There are at least 8,000 infectious disease specialists in the United States.

Take this totally unscientific quiz to find out if infectious disease doctor might be a good career for you.

1 **How are you at solving problems?**
a) I'm great at finding solutions.
b) Sometimes, I have good ideas.
c) You'd better ask someone else.

2 **Are you interested in how the body works?**
a) I read everything I can find about the human body.
b) I think it's sort of interesting.
c) I just try to stay healthy.

3 **Are you good in an emergency?**
a) I always stay calm.
b) I usually keep my head.
c) I jump at any noise.

4 **Do you get grossed out easily?**
a) Never. In fact, I like to watch operations on TV.
b) I don't mind the sight of blood.
c) I feel sick just thinking about that question.

5 **When you go to the doctor, are you curious about your health?**
a) Yes. I ask a lot of questions.
b) Sort of. I want to understand what's wrong with me.
c) No. I just don't want to be sick.

YOUR SCORE
Give yourself 3 points for every "**a**" you chose.
Give yourself 2 points for every "**b**" you chose.
Give yourself 1 point for every "**c**" you chose.

If you got **13–15 points**, you'd probably be a good infectious disease doctor.
If you got **10–12 points**, you might be a good infectious disease doctor.
If you got **5–9 points**, you might want to look at another career!

HOW TO GET STARTED...NOW!

It's never too early to start working toward your goals.

GET AN EDUCATION

▶ Starting now, take as many biology, chemistry, physics, health, and math classes as you can. Train yourself to ask questions, gather new information, and make conclusions the way infectious disease doctors do.

▶ Work on your communication skills. Join the drama club or debate team. It's good practice in thinking before you speak and listening to others.

▶ Start thinking about college. Look for ones that have good science programs. Call or write to those colleges to get information.

▶ Read the newspapers. Keep up with what's happening in our community.

▶ Read anything you can about infectious diseases. Learn about historical and recent cases. See the books and Web sites in the Resources section on pages 56–58.

▶ Graduate from high school!

NETWORK!

▶ Ask your own doctor for advice about becoming an infectious disease doctor.

▶ Get in touch with your local hospital. Ask if you can interview an infectious disease doctor. Maybe spend a day with him or her to get a sense of what the job is like.

GET AN INTERNSHIP

Call your local hospital or doctor's offices. There might be internships or volunteer opportunities available. It doesn't hurt to ask!

LEARN ABOUT OTHER JOBS IN THE FIELD

biologist: studies living organisms

ecologist: studies how organisms relate to the environment

entomologist: specializes in insects

epidemiologist: medical scientist who studies what causes, and how to control, **epidemics**

infectious disease pharmacist: specializes in putting formulas together and dispensing drugs with a focus on infectious disease medicines

microbiologist: studies microscopic cells in human illness

parasitologist: studies parasites

pathologist: studies disease, especially its effects on body tissue

zoologist: specializes in animal life

Resources

Looking for more information about germs and infectious diseases? Here are some you won't want to miss!

PROFESSIONAL ORGANIZATIONS

American Society for Microbiology (ASM)
www.asm.org
1752 N Street, NW
Washington, DC 20036
PHONE: 202-737-3600

The ASM is the world's largest scientific society of individuals interested in the microbiological sciences. Microbiologists study microbes—bacteria, viruses, fungi, algae, and protozoa. Some of these microbes cause diseases. But many of them contribute to the balance of nature or are helpful in other ways. The society's mission is to learn more about microbiology through scientific research.

Infectious Diseases Society of America (IDSA)
www.idsociety.org
66 Canal Center Plaza, Suite 600
Alexandria, VA 22324
PHONE: 703-299-0200
FAX: 703-299-0204
E-MAIL: info@idsociety.org

The IDSA represents physicians, scientists, and other health-care professionals who specialize in infectious diseases. The society's purpose is to improve the health of individuals, communities, and society. The society promotes excellence in patient care, education, research, public health, and prevention relating to infectious diseases.

International Society for Infectious Diseases (ISID)
www.isid.org
1330 Beacon Street, Suite 228
Brookline MA 02446
PHONE: 617-277-0551
FAX: 617-278-9113
E-MAIL: info@isid.org

The ISID tries to improve the care of patients with infectious diseases. It also tries to improve the training of clinicians and researchers in infectious diseases and microbiology. In addition, it tries to control infectious diseases worldwide.

Society of Infectious Disease Pharmacists (SIDP)

www.sidp.org/
823 Congress Avenue, Suite 230
Austin, TX 78701
PHONE: 512-479-0425
FAX: 512-495-9031
E-MAIL: sidp@eami.com

The SIDP provides education, advocacy, and leadership in all aspects of the treatment of infectious diseases. The society is made up of pharmacists and other health-care professionals involved in patient care, research, teaching, drug development, and governmental regulation.

WEB SITES

Mayo Clinic
www.mayoclinic.com
This is a medical site aimed at helping people manage their health.

National Center for Infectious Diseases
www.cdc.gov/ncidod/id_links.htm
Planning to travel to a foreign country? Check out this site to learn how to avoid getting an infectious disease.

National Institute of Allergy and Infectious Disease
www3.niaid.nih.gov/
This site provides the latest research and updates about infectious disease.

National Library of Medicine
www.medlineplus.gov
This is the largest medical library in the world and has information about current studies done on infectious diseases.

Science Magazine Online
www.sciencemag.org
Check out their archives for cool parasite articles and photos.

U.S. Department of Agriculture
www.ars.usda.gov
Look here for updated information about food safety.

Web MD
www.webmd.com
This is a comprehensive, easy-to-use site with all sorts of helpful medical information.

World Health Organization
www.who.int/en/
This international organization offers infectious disease information in English, French, and Spanish.

BOOKS

Brunelle, Lynn, and Barbara Ravage, eds. *Bacteria* (Discovery Channel School Science). Milwaukee: Gareth Stevens Publishing, 2003.

Gave, Marc, and Lynn Brunelle, eds. *Viruses* (Discovery Channel School Science). Milwaukee: Gareth Stevens Publishing, 2003.

Goldstein, Natalie. *Viruses* (Germs! The Library of Disease-Causing Organisms). New York: Rosen Publishing Group, 2004.

Grady, Denise. *Deadly Invaders: Virus Outbreaks Around the World, from Marburg Fever to Avian Flu* (A New York Times Book). New York: Kingfisher, 2006.

Herbst, Judith. *Germ Theory* (Great Ideas of Science). New York: Twenty-First Century Books, 2007.

Latta, Sara J. *The Good, the Bad, the Slimy: The Secret Life of Microbes.* Berkeley Heights, N.J.: Enslow Publishers, 2006.

Monroe, Judy. *Influenza and Other Viruses* (Perspectives on Disease and Illness). Mankato, Minn.: Capstone Press, 2001.

Nardo, Don. *Germs* (Great Medical Discoveries). Minneapolis: Lucent, 2003.

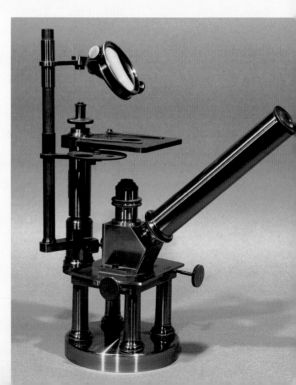

This microscope was used by Louis Pasteur (1822-1895) when he studied bacteria.

A

anesthesia (AN-iss-THEE-zha) *noun* a drug or gas given to people before an operation to prevent them from feeling pain

antibiotic (AN-tee-bye-OT-ik) *noun* a drug that kills bacteria and helps treat infections

B

bacteria (bak-TEER-ee-ah) *noun* single-celled life-forms found in the air, soil, or water, which can cause disease in humans

blood sample (blud SAM-pul) *noun* a small amount of blood taken from a patient, either by poking a finger or placing a needle in a vein. Blood samples are taken to determine if there are organisms in the patient's blood and body.

boils (boylz) *noun* swollen, red sores filled with pus

C

catheter (KATH-uh-tur) *noun* a device used to filter poisons out of the body

cellulitis (sel-yuh-LI-tiss) *noun* a swelling of the skin and deep tissues underneath

coma (KOH-muh) *noun* a state of deep unconsciousness from which it is hard to wake up

CT scan (SEE-tee SKAN) *noun* a device that uses x-rays to look inside the body; also called a CAT scan. It's short for *computerized tomography.*

cultures (KUHL-churs) *noun* samples of bacteria in a petri dish, which scientists study

D

diagnosis (di-ag-NOH-sis) *noun* the identification of a condition or disease

E

epidemics (ep-uh-DEM-iks) *noun* infectious diseases that spread quickly through a population

ER (EE-ahr) *noun* an area in a hospital for patients who need immediate attention. It's short for *emergency room.*

F

folliculitis (FOL-ik-uhl-EYE-tiss) *noun* a condition resulting from an infection that causes tiny white-headed pimples to break out on the skin

I

ICU (eye-SEE-yoo) *noun* an area in a hospital where very ill patients stay. It's short for *intensive care unit*.

immune systems (ih-MYOON SISS-tuhmz) *noun* systems of human bodies that protect people from disease and illness

impetigo (im-peh-TYE-go) *noun* a condition caused from an infection that causes pimple-like sores

incisions (in-SIH-zhunz) *noun* cuts in the skin made by a doctor during surgery

infection (in-FEK-shun) *noun* sickness caused when bacteria or viruses invade the body

infectious disease doctor (in-FEK-shuhss duh-ZEEZ DOK-tur) *noun* a doctor who specializes in diagnosing and treating all kinds of infections

internal medicine doctor (in-TUR-nuhl MED-uh-suhn dok-tur) *noun* this is the first doctor you see in the doctor's office

IV (EYE-vee) *noun* a device for giving medication or fluids through a vein. It's short for *intravenous*.

M

meningitis (men-in-JYE-tiss) *noun* an infection that affects the brain and the nerves

MRI (em-ahr-EYE) *noun* a test that produces computerized images of a patient's body. It's short for *magnetic resonance imaging*.

N

nauseated (NAW-shuss) *adjective* feeling sick to your stomach

necrotizing fasciitis (NEK-roh-TYE-zing fah-SHEYE-tiss) *noun* an illness that feeds on your flesh; also known as the flesh-eating disease

nephrologist (nef-ROL-uh-just) *noun* a doctor who specializes in diseases of the kidneys

neurologist (nuh-ROL-uh-just) *noun* a doctor who treats the brain and nervous system

O

OR (OH-ahr) *noun* an area in a hospital where surgeries are performed. It's short for *operating room*.

P

penicillin (PEN-uh-SIL-un) *noun* a drug originally made from a mold that kills bacteria and helps treat disease

pneumonia (noo-MOH-nyuh) *noun* a serious disease that causes the lungs to fill up with thick fluid and become inflamed, causing serious problems with breathing

R

resistant (ri-ZIS-tunt) *adjective* able to fight off something; not affected by something

S

scalded skin syndrome (SKAWLD-id skin SIN-drohm) *noun* a staph infection that turns into a rash all over the body and causes the skin to peel off

scarlet fever (SKAR-lit FEE-vur) *noun* a rash made up of tiny red pinpoints that can follow a case of strep throat

staph (staf) *noun* a common bacteria carried on skin and in noses. It's short for *Staphylococcus*.

strep (strep) *noun* a common bacteria that can cause infection and illness, including strep throat. It's short for *Streptococcus*.

U

ultrasound (UHL-truh-sound) *noun* an examination using a device that sends sound waves into an injured area in order to create an image of the infected area

Index

oxacillin, 47

parasitologists, 55
Pasteur, Louis, 47, *47*
pathologists, 55
penicillin, 23, 40, 46
petri dishes, 23, 50, *50*
pneumonia, 10, 37, 37, 38, 43, *44*
pus cultures, 21, 39

questions, 14, 18, 29, 37
quiz, 54

resistance, 9, 32, 40, 41, 48, 49

salary, 53
Salisbury, Bo, 16, 18–19, 20–21,
    22, 23, 24, 25–26
scalded skin syndrome, 11, *11*
scarlet fever, 11, *11*
slides, 50, *50*
staph, 9, 10, 11, 21, 23, 31, 32,
    38, 39, 40, *40*, 43–44, *44*,
    47, 48, 49
sterilization, 47, *47*, 49, *49*, 51
strep, 9, 10, 11, 21, *21*, 22, 26
strep throat, 9, 11, 22
Streptococcus pyrogenes, 21
superbugs, 40, 41, 42, 47, *47*,
    48, 49
surgery, 9, 10, 21, 24, 29, *29*,
    31, 33, *33*
syringes, 50, *50*, 51

toxins, 22

ultrasound, 21
universal precautions, 51
University of California, Davis
    Medical Center, 19
urine tests, 21, 30, *31*, 39

vancomycin, 40, 42, 47
ventilator machines, 12, 37, *37*,
    41, *42*

Washington Redskins football team,
    49, *49*

Woodland Hills, California, 36, *36*
World War II, 46

x-ray machines, 51, *51*

zoologists, 55

Author's Note

Researching this book was especially important to me because I once witnessed a staph infection case close-up. I know firsthand how serious they are.

Here's my story: In January 2002, I drove my husband, Peter, to the emergency room at a nearby hospital. After days of fever and vomiting, he was experiencing extreme abdominal pain. It turned out that, due to a previously undetected genetic condition, his stomach had pushed its way into his esophagus, causing him to bleed internally. "I don't think he's going to make it," the emergency room doctor warned as they rushed him into emergency surgery.

Hours later Peter was wheeled into the Intensive Care Unit. The surgery had been successful. Little did I realize, however, that the worst was yet to come.

Complications arose by the hour. He had pneumonia. His stomach wasn't functioning. The medication, especially the morphine, made him itchy, irritable, and hallucinatory. (He demanded we throw a party for everyone in the ICU, serve cocktail wieners, and watch videos.)

Peter's case was being monitored by a host of specialists: a cardiologist to manage his heart functions, a pulmonary specialist to oversee his lungs, a gastroenterologist for his stomach ailments, and the operating surgeon for his post-operative care.

But it was the onset of a surgical staph infection that pushed Peter's case back to serious. None of the specialists made a move without talking with the infectious disease doctor who became the lead doctor on the case. At this stage, the highest priority for everyone was to eliminate the staph infection. Staph was clearly an unwelcome and threatening invader.

Thankfully, there's a happy ending. Peter's staph infection and pneumonia were cured with antibiotics, and his surgical wound healed nicely. After three weeks in intensive care, and two weeks in another ward, he was released. Today he's healthy and has never since requested a cocktail wiener.

ACKNOWLEDGMENTS

I would like to thank the following people. Without their help, this book would not be possible.

Dr. Pamela Nagami
Dr. Tiffany Grunwald
Dr. Rekha Murthy
Dr. Michael Flagg
Thomas D. Lewis
Shelly Fredman
Dr. Lisa Chan Flagg

CONTENT ADVISER: Mark S. Dworkin, MD, MPH and TM, Associate Professor, Division of Epidemiology and Biostatistics, University of Illinois at Chicago